Everglades National Park

PRESERVING AMERICA

Nate Frisch

Published by
CREATIVE EDUCATION

P.O. Box 227, Mankato, Minnesota 56002
Creative Education is an imprint of The Creative Company
www.thecreativecompany.us

Design and production by Danny Nanos of Gilbert & Nanos
Art direction by Rita Marshall
Printed in the United States of America

Photographs by Alamy (J. Greenberg/Photri Images), Shutterstock (John A. Anderson,
Walter G. Arce, Jeff Banke, Alita Bobrov, George Burba, ChipPix, jo Crebbin, FloridaStock,
Jonathan G, IgorGolovniov, jeff gynane, holbox, iofoto, eduard ionesco, Jesse Kunerth,
Philip Lange, Larsek, Leighton Photography & Imaging, Mikhail Levit, National Parks Service,
pandapaw, pashabo, Jose Antonio Perez, A. Petelin, Jason Patrick Ross, Henryk Sadura,
William Silver, Stocksnapper, TEA, Matt Tilghman, Maxim Tupikov,
Rudy Umans, MANSILIYA YURY)

Library of Congress Cataloging-in-Publication Data

Frisch, Nate.
Everglades National Park / by Nate Frisch.
p. cm. — (Preserving America)
Includes bibliographical references and index.
Summary: An exploration of Everglades National Park, including how its wetlands-rich landscape was formed,
its history of preservation, and tourist attractions such as the bus route called Tram Road.

ISBN 978-1-60818-195-7
1. Everglades National Park (Fla.)—Juvenile literature. I. Title.
F317.E9F74 2013
975.9'39—dc23   2012023229

2 4 6 8 9 7 5 3

Cover & page 3: *An Everglades slough along Tamiami Trail; a flamingo*

CREATIVE EDUCATION

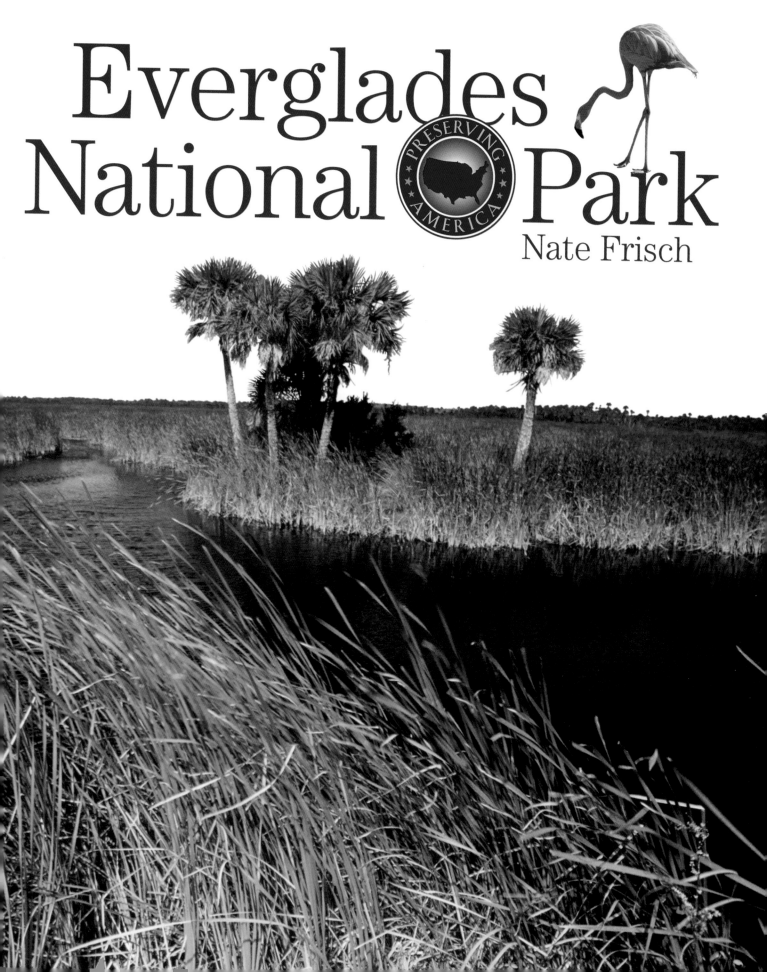

Everglades
National Park

Nate Frisch

Table of Contents

TOWERING MOUNTAINS and glassy lakes. Churning rivers and dense forests. Lush prairies and baking deserts. The open spaces and natural wonders of the United States once seemed as limitless as they were diverse. But as human expansion and development increased in the 1800s, forests and prairies were replaced by settlements and agricultural lands. Waterways were diverted, wildlife was over-hunted, and the earth was scarred by mining. Fortunately, many Americans fought to preserve some of the country's vanishing wilderness. In 1872, Yellowstone National Park was established, becoming the first true national park in the world and paving the way for future preservation efforts. In 1901, Theodore Roosevelt became U.S. president. He once stated, "There can be no greater issue than that of conservation in this country," and during his presidency, Roosevelt signed five national parks into existence. The National Park Service (NPS) was created in 1916 to manage the growing number of U.S. parks. In 1947, America's collection of preserved wildernesses came to include Everglades National Park, in southern Florida. Featuring vast wetlands and an assortment of wildlife found nowhere else in the country, this subtropical preserve immediately earned a place among America's most fascinating parks.

A Misfit Landscape

In many respects, the Everglades seems an odd fit in the U.S. The land, the water, the plant life, and the animals of this expansive wetland simply don't fit the typical mold of an American national park. In fact, they don't fit the mold of American landscapes, habitats, or anything else. The explanation for the Everglades' uniqueness begins with the state in which it is found.

On a map of the U.S., the **peninsular** state of Florida seems out of place, and in a way, it is. All of the continents on Earth are moving and have been for millions of years in a process called continental drift. About 300 million years ago, land that later became known as Africa collided with what is now North America. Before the collision, the land that is today Florida was likely attached to the African landmass. The slow but incredibly powerful impact of the two continents created the Appalachian Mountains of North America and the Anti-Atlas Mountains of northern Africa. During the same impact, Florida broke free of Africa. About 180 million years ago, the continents began to separate again, and Florida remained attached to North America.

This does not directly explain why the Everglades features plants and animals found nowhere else in the U.S., because in the many millions of years since then, life forms have come and gone, and nearly any living thing that inhabited Florida 300 million years ago is long extinct. However, Florida's southerly location and exposure to the Atlantic Ocean and Gulf of Mexico support **ecosystems** unique to the Everglades. The region is at the junction of

Compared with most national parks, the flat Everglades is shockingly low in elevation; Rock Reef Pass is actually a high point

Rock Reef Pass
Elevation 3 feet

temperate North America and the tropical Caribbean, which creates a
region called the subtropics that hosts ecosystems and life forms
characteristic of both. The Everglades also has distinct wet and dry
seasons that further define the landscape and wildlife.

But the primary reason for the Everglades' watery ecosystem is
its low, flat terrain. Elevation throughout this vast region rarely varies
more than 20 feet (6 m), and for several periods over the past millions
of years, the Everglades has been under a shallow ocean. In fact, the
rock bed beneath the Everglades is primarily limestone, a stone that is
composed of ancient shellfish remains. Today, the land is barely above
sea level, and water continues to define the region.

The Everglades begins as far north as Lake Okeechobee and

*Everglades summers
are hot and humid, but
visitors who brave the
conditions see the
wilderness when it is
most lush and green*

11

extends south to the very tip of Florida. The large but shallow Lake Okeechobee is fed by the Kissimmee River and is the primary source of the Everglades river system, which does not contain distinct, identifiable rivers but rather is an enormous floodplain. Since Okeechobee has an elevation of only 14 feet (4 m), and the ocean it drains into can be 100 miles (161 km) away, the drainage routes have virtually no slope. During the wet season, which lasts from May to November, the overflowing Lake Okeechobee and frequent rain showers create a sprawling, 50-mile-wide (80 km) stream that is often no more than a few feet (1 m) deep and in some places flows only about 100 feet (30 m) downstream per day. This slow water movement is known as sheetflow.

Perhaps the most dominant life form in the region is the Everglades' sawgrass. This reedy, grasslike plant takes its name from the small, sawlike notches along the edge of the leaf blades, and it grows out of shallow, slow-moving water throughout the Everglades. It tends to grow densely over broad areas where few other plants or animals exist. In fact, an expansive area south of Lake Okeechobee is called the Sawgrass Plains, and the widespread presence of the plant has earned the Everglades the descriptive nickname "River of Grass."

However, these sawgrass-filled marshes are just one of several ecosystems in the Everglades. Slightly deeper areas of water are

called sloughs. Often found amid the flooded prairies are tropical hardwood hammocks. These are small islands whose elevation is just high enough to avoid seasonal flooding, and they feature a variety of tropical plants as well as large trees such as oaks, royal palms, and West Indies mahoganies. Land areas that are a little higher and drier still are called pinelands due to the presence of slash pines. Along the southern and western coasts of the Everglades are mangrove swamps. Mangrove trees are able to survive in **brackish** water and poor soil, and their extensive root systems allow them to endure severe tropical storms and the constant wearing effect of the ocean's waves. The resilient trees also form a protective barrier for areas farther inland. Florida Bay, which is part of the ocean beyond the southern mangrove swamp, is also considered one of the Everglades' ecosystems, since that is where the inland water eventually drains. This saltwater, marine environment supports various types of algae and sea grasses.

Because of the varied amounts, depths, and types of water and the range of plant life it supports, the Everglades features a vast and diverse array of animal life described as aquatic, **terrestrial**, **arboreal**, or some combination of these. No animals are more iconic than the region's alligators and crocodiles, but other high-profile species include

Two of the most iconic plants of the Everglades, sawgrass (left) and mangrove shrubs (right) are small in size but vast in numbers

The Florida softshell turtle, which is surprisingly speedy, is 1 of the 16 turtle or tortoise species at home in the Everglades

sea turtles, West Indian manatees, and cougars called Florida panthers. The various ecosystems also support many snakes, wading birds, frogs, and fish. In total, more than 50 species of reptiles, 40 mammals, 350 birds, 15 amphibians, and 300 fish are found in the Everglades.

The presence and activity of life within the Everglades is often dictated by the wet and dry cycles of the area's climate. The wet season occurs from May through November and sees nearly 80 percent of the Everglades' annual 50 to 60 inches (127–152 cm) of rainfall. During this time, much of the landscape is covered by water, and even large terrestrial animals such as white-tailed deer and panthers are mostly confined to the small hardwood hammocks, while aquatic creatures have the run of the Everglades.

During the dry season, the ecosystems shift. Instead of miles and miles of water dotted with occasional pockets of dry land, the Everglades features miles and miles of solid ground with occasional water holes. This dry season results in dense concentrations of animal life, as aquatic animals congregate in what limited streams and pools remain, and most terrestrial creatures cannot stray far from these sources of drinking water.

This climatic cycle has been in place for several thousand years, but some of the first human inhabitants of the Everglades saw yet another form of the region. Around 15,000 years ago, the last **ice age** had not yet ended. While glaciers did not reach the Everglades, the region was a cool

desert inhabited by now extinct animals including saber-toothed cats, giant sloths, and spectacled bears. It is likely that **nomadic** human hunters ended up in Florida by following such large animals. Within the last 10,000 years, climate changes have made the region into the watery landscape it is today.

Crocodiles (pictured) and alligators look similar, but "crocs" have V-shaped snouts, whereas "gators" have U-shaped ones

Saving the Great Wetland

Beginning about 5,000 years ago, larger tribes took up permanent residence near the Everglades. The two most prominent were the Calusa in the west and the Tequesta in the east. The two groups had limited contact with one another, but the available resources and watery surroundings made their ways of life very similar. Both fed on fish, shellfish, plants, and the mammals—including deer—they hunted. The area's limestone was too fragile to be useful in making tools, so the natives instead used seashells, wood, and animal bones and teeth for items such as arrowheads and blades. The tribes built canoes, which they used to travel through the Everglades and even to Cuba, a large island nearly 100 miles (161 km) south of Florida. They also built canals to channel fresh water from the Everglades to their drier villages near the coasts.

Many prehistoric reptiles and marine life forms called the land now known as Florida home, leaving behind an array of fossils

The cultures of the Calusa, Tequesta, and various smaller tribes went relatively undisturbed until Spanish explorers reached Florida in 1513. At that time, more than 10,000 natives may have lived in the region, and although the Everglades' abundant water and plant and animal life were of great value to the tribes living there, the Spaniards—who were mainly interested in gold and other riches—saw little use for the swampy land. Nonetheless, the encounter represented a kind of death knell, as European influence soon caused the drastic decline of American Indian cultures and populations.

Heavily armed Spanish explorers called conquistadors tried to subdue and enslave the tribes of Florida, with varying success. Some tribes were quickly defeated, but others retreated deeper into the Everglades, where the Spaniards were reluctant to follow. Still, many

Indians who were not killed in battle died from diseases—such as yellow fever, smallpox, and measles—brought from Europe. And as Indian tribes such as the Creek were pushed from their longtime home-lands in the north, they drifted into the Everglades, where they fought with the resident tribes over the shrinking pockets of land that were not controlled by Europeans.

By the mid-1700s, most of the region's American Indian population had died or relocated to islands off the Florida coast. Those who remained in the Everglades were a mixed group composed of Calusas, Tequestas, and other southern Florida tribes that had been absorbed into the invading tribes from the north. Collectively, this group of native peoples became known as the Seminoles.

The scarily-named Snake Bight is one of the Everglades' many bights—a bay within a larger bay (in this case, Florida Bay)

From 1763 to 1783, control of Florida shifted from the Spanish to the British and back to the Spanish. In the War of 1812, the U.S.—having recently won its independence from Britain—fought against its former motherland. In battles that took place in and near Florida, Britain recruited Seminole warriors, including "black Seminoles"—runaway slaves who had found refuge among the tribe. British troops were forced out of the U.S. in 1815, and over the next few years, U.S. soldiers invaded Florida, which was still governed by Spain. Florida and the Everglades became part of the U.S. in 1821, but conflicts with the Seminoles continued until 1858. By the time the last of three "Seminole Wars" had ended, most of the Seminole nation had been relocated onto reservations.

Initially in southern Florida, only a small number of white settlements sprang up on the land taken from the Seminoles. These early settlements were limited to the drier coasts, just as native villages had been. To make the land more suitable for settlement and development, plans to drain the Everglades were put into action in the 1880s. Huge drainage canals were dug to divert water away from the Everglades. The artificial drainage created more dry land, and coastal villages including Chokoloskee, Cape Sable, and Flamingo were established. Village buildings were often constructed on stilts as a precaution against perennial flooding, and the swampy interior of southern Florida was still considered worthless to most people.

Alligators have long been viewed as a kind of fashion resource, as the animals' skin has been used to make boots, wallets, and more

The interior's few residents were called Gladesmen and spent much of their time in small boats, surviving in the

wilderness by fishing and hunting animals such as alligators, deer, and otters. The animals provided not only food to eat but food and hides to sell or trade. But while most Gladesmen hunted to survive, other hunters killed animals primarily for profit. In the late 1800s and early 1900s, millions of alligators, otters, birds, and other animals were killed for their skins, furs, and feathers. Feathers in particular were prized as adornments for women's hats, and the vibrant plumage of Everglades birds such as egrets led to their slaughter.

By the start of the 20th century, the controlled draining of the Everglades had slowed. Then, in 1904, **gubernatorial** candidate Napoleon Bonaparte Broward based his campaign largely on a pledge to drain the Everglades to create huge expanses of dry land for development. Broward won the election, and his plans went into effect in 1905. As more water was diverted via canals, swamps became agricultural land or sites for new towns. Over the next decade, the growing presence of newly invented automobiles and the roads they required led to

This 1880 illustration depicts the Everglades wetlands and some of the birds that were pursued at the time for their feathers

additional drainage. Local railways were also constructed during that time, further impacting the landscape and bringing more people to the developing region.

Some Floridians who witnessed the transformation of the Everglades began to recognize the need to protect at least some of the land and the life within it. In 1901, in an early step toward local conservation, the state of Florida had banned the hunting of birds for their feathers, and a local wilderness guide named Guy Bradley was hired as the Everglades' bird warden and deputy sheriff. Bradley was passionate about nature and his job but was greeted with hostility by many hunters. Illegal bird hunting persisted, and in 1905, Bradley was murdered by a hunter after arresting the man's son for poaching. Ultimately, it was the banned sales of bird plumage in New York that halted bird hunting in Florida. Meanwhile, the hunting of other Everglades animals continued unchecked. In the early 1910s, a hunter reportedly killed 250 alligators and 172 otters during a single trip into the wetlands. In 1916, Royal Palm State Park was created near Homestead in southeastern Florida. Hunting there was outlawed, but the park covered just a little more than six square miles (15 sq km)—not even 1 percent of the Everglades.

Even though hunting continued to take a high toll on wildlife populations, it was land development that remained the Everglades' biggest threat. Southern Florida's tropical features and warm climate were unique among U.S. destinations, and in the 1920s, tourists began flocking to growing cities such as Miami and Fort Lauderdale on the eastern seashore and Fort Myers on the western shore. This, in turn, led to more canals and more roads. Dense mangrove trees along the shorelines were torn out and replaced with palm trees that were more appealing to tourists and didn't block ocean views.

Local naturalists watched these developments with alarm, and by 1923, some people were proposing the creation of an Everglades national park. Support for the idea was growing when, in 1928, hurricanes in southern Florida caused Lake Okeechobee and canals to overflow, and thousands of people were killed. That same year, the Florida state legislature created both the Okeechobee Flood Control District and the Tropical Everglades National Park Commission—programs that struck many people as contradictory. The first led to the construction of the Herbert Hoover Dike, a human-made, damlike shoreline that regulated any water flow from Lake Okeechobee into the Everglades, while the second considered the possible formation of a national park that would preserve part of the Everglades in its natural state.

One of the creatures Ernest F. Coe wanted to protect was the great white heron, a wading bird with a seven-foot (2.1 m) wingspan

Ernest F. Coe, a land developer-turned-conservationist, emerged as the leader of the Tropical Everglades National Park Commission. The more than 3,000 square miles (7,770 sq km) he proposed to turn into a national park was considered unreasonably large by many Floridians, including land developers and hunters. Despite protests, on May 30, 1934, the U.S. Congress authorized the establishment of Everglades National Park. It was a victory for conservation, but it carried significant limitations. No funds would be available to follow through with its creation for several years, and the park would include about 2,300 square miles (5,957 sq km)—only two-thirds of the land Coe had wanted.

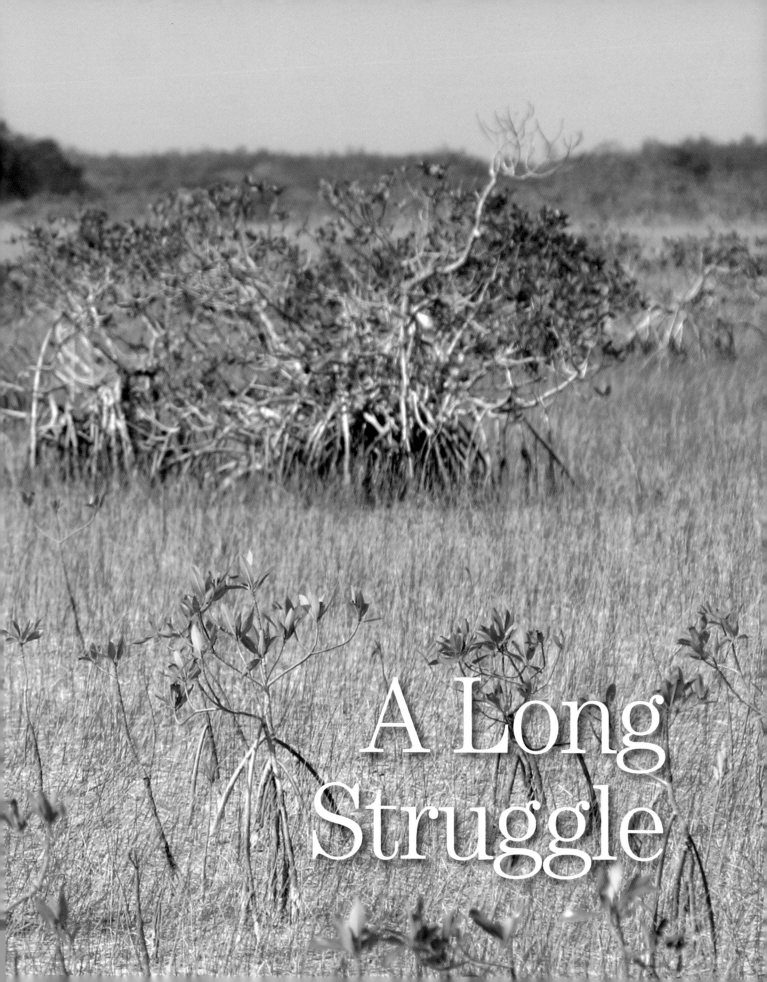

A Long
Struggle

Even after Everglades National Park was green-lighted as a protected area in 1934, a long struggle followed as conservationists and the region—which was not immediately a functioning national park—faced a host of serious obstacles. The limited funding made available for the young park was used to slowly buy pockets of land that had been privately owned by Gladesmen or other Everglades residents. This left almost nothing to be spent on the construction of park roads and facilities or on the monitoring of illegal hunting within the park's borders. Another challenge stemmed from the fact that the park included less than a quarter of the original Everglades, and it was at the very southern end of the region. This meant that park officials could create all the in-park conservation policies they wanted to return the land to its natural state, but the park's water came from the tightly regulated Lake Okeechobee and had to flow south through 70 miles (113 km) of unprotected land filled with canals.

Early on, little water was allowed through the Lake Okeechobee **levee**, and much of the Everglades became too dry. In 1939, widespread wildfires destroyed hundreds of square miles of vegetation. After World War II (1939–45), the population of southern Florida increased dramatically, and more buildings, roads, and canals were built in the unrestricted parts of the Everglades.

Then, in 1947, Marjory Stoneman Douglas published *The Everglades: River of Grass*. Douglas was a former reporter for the *Miami Herald* newspaper, and she had dedicated herself to studying

the Everglades for several years. Her book reported on the wondrous ecosystems she had come to know in this amazing expanse of America and the damage they were sustaining due to human activity, and it publicized the need for further conservation like never before. On December 6, 1947, U.S. president Harry Truman dedicated Everglades National Park, and the park officially opened.

In 1948, the U.S. Congress authorized a new water-control plan in the Everglades. Before then, new canals and roads were built with little consideration given to the larger scheme of things; the new plan would redevelop canals, roads, and levees as part of a comprehensive water-control system. In theory, this would provide developed areas with adequate drinking water and flood protection while also leaving an ample water supply for Everglades National Park. The system proved more efficient than the haphazard maze of canals and roads that had preceded it, but it benefited the developed areas more than the natural ones. Not enough water was being allowed to reach Everglades National Park, and by the 1960s, aquatic ecosystems within the park were drying up. In that same decade, the U.S. government proposed plans to build a huge international airport just north of Everglades National Park—a development that would have required additional water restrictions to keep the facilities and necessary roads protected from floods.

However, the end of the 1960s saw a resurgence of conservationism in Florida. The airport proposal was defeated, and in 1972, Congress passed a bill that limited future developments in parts of southern

With his 1947 dedication of the park, President Truman officially gave much-needed protection to Florida's sprawling wetlands

Florida and ordered more water to be allowed to reach the national park. Nearby sections of land and water also gained some measure of protection, which consequently also helped the national park. Most notable was the 1974 creation of the Big Cypress National Preserve, an area almost half the size of the national park and immediately to its north.

Even with the new legislation and protected "buffer" zones, Everglades National Park remained at the mercy of whatever happened upstream toward Lake Okeechobee and the ever-growing metropolitan areas along southern Florida's shorelines. In 1989, the Everglades National Park Protection and Expansion Act was passed to once again demand that adequate water be allowed to reach the national park— something that had not been carried out as described in the 1972 bill. This bill, signed by president George H. W. Bush, also added 171 square miles (443 sq km) of land to the eastern edge of the national park and banned the in-park use of airboats, whose loud engines were disruptive to wildlife.

One of the Everglades' more than 50 butterfly species, the palamedes swallowtail thrives in swampy habitats and wet woods

Perhaps not surprisingly, the 1989 legislation still wasn't sufficient. Most water continued to be diverted to Florida's eastern and western shores, and the water that reached Everglades National Park did not arrive in a natural, wide, sheetlike river as it once did. Besides water quantities, water *quality* was also an issue. By way of the processes of collection and diversion, water contaminated with agricultural herbicides and pesticides ended up in the national park. And ocean salt water followed canals inland where it would not naturally occur, killing freshwater plants, fish, and other animals as a result.

In 2000, the Comprehensive Everglades Restoration Project (CERP) began. CERP was a multifaceted plan to improve both the

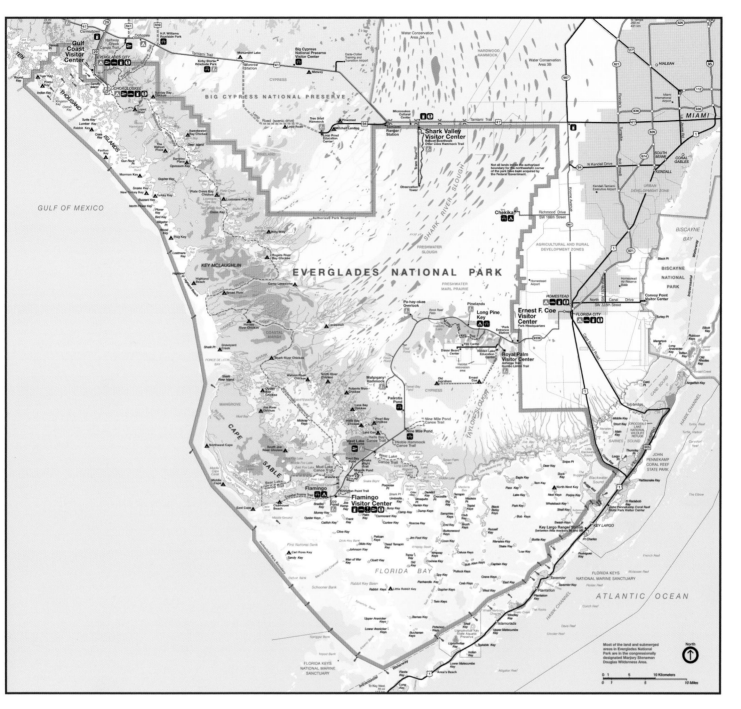

quality and quantity of water in the Everglades region. However, the multibillion-dollar plan carried a timeline exceeding 30 years, which hardly seemed promising to conservation groups that had long grown weary of unfulfilled promises and unsuccessful plans for the Everglades' protection. CERP consisted of about 60 smaller projects that involved

This map of Everglades National Park illustrates the sprawl of the wilderness area across southern Florida

29

In places, cypress trees dominate the Everglades landscape, as these trees can grow out of ground that is either dry or waterlogged

such tasks as the collection of extra water for the Everglades, the removal of agricultural chemicals from soil, and evaluations of the best times to release stored water. Several of these small projects were given a five-year timeline, but as of 2012, only one had been completed.

Today, nearly 40 animal species whose populations have diminished are federally protected within the park. These include American crocodiles, sea turtles, Florida panthers, and manatees. In every case, habitat loss is the main factor in their decline. Studies on the park's various wading birds, including storks and herons, showed that their numbers dropped 90 percent between 1940 and 2000. Such birds play a valuable role in the ecosystem by helping maintain balanced populations among the smaller aquatic animals that they eat.

Water issues aside, possibly the greatest problem facing the Everglades today is the ongoing invasion of nonnative plant and animal species. The unwanted introduction of species into habitats in which they do not naturally occur is common throughout the U.S. and in other national parks, but the Everglades' warm climate, close proximity to urban areas, and unique mixture of land and water habitats make it especially prone to invasive species.

Invasive plants in the Everglades tend to smother native plant life, which causes **monocultures** and affects the animals that rely on native plants for food or shelter. One such example is the latherleaf. Originally from Asia, this bush has creeping, vinelike branches that grow over lower plants and choke out young pines, oaks, and other trees. This reduces the variety of plant food available and narrows the shelter and nesting locations for animals such as squirrels and songbirds. As those small animals are reduced in number, so too are the larger animals—such as hawks and foxes—that prey upon them. Today, park officials combat areas of latherleaf and other unwanted plant growth by burning, cutting, uprooting, or chemically treating them.

An ongoing problem in and around the Everglades is the release of pets or livestock into the wild. The park's invasive animal species include **feral** dogs, cats, and pigs, as well as more exotic pets such as pythons, boa constrictors, and a long list of lizards. These nonnative creatures not only threaten the plants or animals they eat but the native animals with which they compete as well. For example, feral dogs and cats will eat many of the same small animals that native bobcats, gray foxes, and—to a lesser extent—endangered Florida panthers prey upon. Today, efforts are being made to trap and remove non-native animals from the Everglades, and programs have been set up to allow owners of exotic pets to turn in their unwanted animals rather than release them into the wild.

Because of Everglades National Park's challenging and unresolved problems regarding water supply, nearby urban sprawl, and invasive species, it is considered by many ecological organizations to be the most threatened park in America's national park system.

Owing to its small population, shy nature, and primarily nocturnal behavior, the Florida panther is a seldom-seen Everglades hunter

By Tram
or by Kayak

In the past decade, Everglades National Park has received approximately one million visitors per year. This attendance is modest compared with that of national parks such as Great Smoky Mountains or Yellowstone, and it can be largely attributed to the park's location. Although close to big metropolitan areas such as Miami, the Everglades compete with wildly popular tourist magnets such as Walt Disney World and Universal Studios. And because Everglades National Park is at the southern tip of Florida, visitors can come from only one direction.

Climate also plays a role in limiting Everglades visitors. In contrast to most national parks, the five busiest months for tourism in the Everglades are the winter and spring months of December, January, February, March, and April. The reason is that temperatures during these months, on average, are a comfortable 50 to 80 °F (10–27 °C). This also happens to be Florida's dry season, and the limited water supply throughout the park causes animals to congregate in fewer areas,

From left to right, Everglades birds: flamingo, great white heron, tricolored heron, black-crowned night heron, great blue heron

which makes bird-watching and wildlife viewing easier. The cooler, drier conditions also drastically reduce the number of mosquitoes and biting flies, which can be horrendous in Florida's hot and humid summers.

Most Everglades tourists visit for the sake of seeing the unique landscape and the life it contains. A single road—appropriately called the Main Park Road—cuts through the park, and another skirts the northern border, so while vehicles are necessary to get from place to place in the nearly 2,500-square-mile (6,475 sq km) park, visitors generally have to leave their cars if they want a fulfilling park experience. The particular type of experience they receive depends on which areas of the park they visit.

Everglades has four main visitor centers scattered across the park. The popular Ernest F. Coe Visitor Center is on the eastern border of the park and along the Main Park Road. The center offers various ranger-led tours and programs, and the center at nearby Royal Palm state park has informative exhibits, a bookshop, and access to the well-traveled Anhinga Trail and Gumbo Limbo Trail. Each of these trails is less than a mile (1.6 km) round trip and provides easy walking on paved or board-walk paths. The Anhinga Trail winds through a sawgrass marsh and offers some of the best opportunities for spotting wildlife such as alligators, turtles, fish, and many birds including herons, egrets, and the anhingas that give the trail its name. The Gumbo Limbo Trail is named after the gumbo limbo trees along this shaded, junglelike path, which also features royal palms, strangler figs, and various ferns.

Following the Main Park Road west and south will lead to various picnic sites and other trails including Long Pine Key Trails, Pineland Trail, Pahayokee Overlook, and Mahogany Hammock Trail. Long Pine Key Trails is a system of paths covering nearly 30 miles (48 km).

Some of the best bird-watching in the Everglades' interior is done from the seat of a canoe or kayak

Bicycles are permitted on these trails and make the longer distance much more manageable. The other three trails are each under a mile (1.6 km) round trip and lead through various types of vegetation including pines, palmettos, wildflowers, sawgrass, and mahoganies.

The Main Park Road ends near the southwestern tip of the Everglades (and the state of Florida, for that matter) at Flamingo Visitor Center. Snake Bight Trail and Eco Pond Trail are common hikes near Flamingo. Both are popular for bird-watching, and crocodiles are occasionally seen at Eco Pond. Other hiking and biking trails are also nearby, but the Flamingo area is best known for its boat tours and boating opportunities. Boat tours run year round, and the visitor's water-going options include trips to the wide-open Florida Bay or to the inland

Whitewater Bay, which is lined by dense clusters of mangrove trees.

Aside from the boat tours, the Flamingo Marina also rents canoes and kayaks. Paddlers can cover the same water as the tour boats but also can choose from among many other designated canoe trails of varying length. Because paddlers can reach a variety of aquatic habitats, they have chances to see a wide range of animals including crocodiles, manatees, black bears, and birds of many sizes, shapes, and colors. Ironically, flamingos are not very common in the area.

Near the northern border of Everglades National Park along the Tamiami Trail road is the Shark Valley Visitor Center. Shark Valley is named after the Shark River, but the area does not have sharks. What it does have is an excellent representation of the Everglades' "river of grass." Most of the park's water passes near Shark Valley, and much of this water is covered by sawgrass. The area features a couple short hiking trails, but the main attraction is the Tram Road. This 15-mile (24 km) loop is not accessible by car, but open-sided buses (trams) provide narrated tours of the loop year round. Along the route, expanses

Kayaks are a great way for solo travelers or small groups to explore the water, as they are easier to paddle and maneuver than canoes

of sawgrass are broken up by pockets of trees and other dry-land vegetation, and alligators, wading birds, **raptors**, and deer are commonly seen. Halfway around the loop is an observation tower that provides panoramic views of the vast, flat terrain below. The trams offer good visibility, but as an alternative, visitors can ride bicycles around the paved Tram Road.

Airboats, banned throughout most of the park, are loud but pose little danger to swimming reptiles, as the boats ride above the water

Driving west from Shark Valley takes guests to the Gulf Coast Visitor Center. This area lacks hiking trails, and the focus is instead on the many waterways found along the shoreline. The nearby area called Ten Thousand Islands is named for the abundance of mangrove islands that exist between the Gulf of Mexico and the Florida mainland. Boat tours navigate this maze to reach the Gulf, where tourists may see dolphins, manatees, and bald eagles. Other tours stay within the mangrove forests, where alligators and mammals such as bobcats and raccoons are more likely to be seen. As in Flamingo, canoes and kayaks can be rented near the Gulf Coast Visitor Center. Reservations for rentals and tours are recommended at both locations.

Freshwater and saltwater fishing are available throughout many areas of Everglades National Park, and anglers may catch snapper, sea trout, redfish, bass, and bluegill, among other fish species. Shorelines are typically not well-suited for fishing, and boat fishing is generally more successful. Florida fishing licenses are needed, and visitors should be aware that freshwater and saltwater fishing require separate licenses.

Overnight accommodations in Everglades National Park are limited. No indoor lodging is available (though it can be found in nearby towns such as Homestead and Everglades City), and only two drive-in campgrounds exist within the park. Long Pine Key Campground is located near the Ernest F. Coe Visitor Center and offers about 100 sites for RVs or tents. Flamingo Campground features more than 200 drive-in sites for RVs and tents, plus 40 walk-in sites. Both campgrounds provide bathrooms and running water, and campsites have picnic tables and fire rings. Neither has RV hookups, and only Flamingo offers showers. Flamingo accepts reservations, and they are strongly recommended for that campground. Everglades also offers **backcountry** campsites that can be reached only by boat. Such sites are found throughout much of the western portion of the park along inland canoe trails or on the small islands along the Gulf Coast. Permits required for these areas can be obtained at the Flamingo and Gulf Coast visitor centers.

The lack of modern conveniences within Everglades National Park is seen by most conservationists as a good thing—an indication of the effort being made to restore and preserve this distinctive landscape. Whether the Everglades' remarkable creatures and ecosystems are still around generations from now depends not only on the NPS but on the ecological decisions made by local governments throughout southern Florida. As such, this park's story serves as a reminder that natural preservation is often a struggle without an end.

Although the Everglades is not as easy to access as many national parks, its unique wilderness has captivated visitors for decades

Many people associate pine trees with northern climates, but the Everglades' bountiful slash pines often surround camping sites

Symbol of the Everglades

When many people think of the Everglades, they think of alligators, reptiles that commonly grow to 12 feet (3.7 m) or longer and can weigh as much as half a ton (450 kg). These descendants from the dinosaur age have broad, rounded snouts, and their scaly skin may be olive, brown, or gray. Although alligators come to dry land to lay eggs and occasionally warm up in the sun, they are most at home in water, where they eat fish, turtles, and nearly any other animal they can catch. In dry seasons, alligators dig out water holes that trap fish and attract other animals as large as deer for the "gators" to prey upon.

Florida's Reclusive Prowler

Elsewhere in North America, they may be called mountain lions, cougars, pumas, or catamounts, but in Florida, they are known as panthers. These typically tan big cats can weigh up to 130 pounds (59 kg) and feed mostly on large mammals such as deer and feral hogs. Smaller mammals and even young alligators also make up a portion of their diet. Florida panthers' only natural predator is large alligators,

but over-hunting and habitat loss have reduced the cat's range and population. Once inhabiting several southeastern states, Florida panthers are now limited to the Everglades and other parts of southern Florida, and only about 100 remain in the wild today.

Everglades in a Day

Everglades tourists with limited time may be best served by driving the Tamiami Trail. Heading from east to west, the first stop should be Shark Valley, where tourists will take the two-hour tram tour that highlights the Everglades' flooded prairies. Farther west, drivers can peel off the main road onto the alternative scenic route in Big Cypress National Preserve to get a taste of the Everglades' forests. This route rejoins the main road before reaching the Gulf Coast Visitor Center, where a Ten Thousand Islands boat tour will cover mangrove swamps and open Gulf waters. Visitors starting out from the west would reverse the sequence of activities.

A Rare Long Hike

The majority of Everglades National Park's walking trails are less than a mile (1.6 km) in length. Visitors who want a little more exercise or to get a bit farther from the crowds might choose the Long Pine Key Trail. Because of the flat terrain, the hike is not difficult, but it covers seven miles (11 km) of pine forests, palm forests, prairies, and small lakes. Alligators, deer, wildflowers, and a wide variety of birds are commonly seen along this trail. Several other trails branch off the main route, offering more opportunities for exercise and sightseeing. Bicycles are also permitted on these trails.

An Even Wetter Destination

*Due east of Everglades National Park and off Florida's eastern coast is Biscayne National Park. This park contains relatively little dry land and instead encompasses a vibrant section of the Atlantic Ocean that features clear blue waters, **coral reefs**, dolphins, whales, various sea plants and crustaceans, and more than 500 species of fish. The area also has an intriguing history involving pirates, shipwrecks, and early explorers. Biscayne's dry season occurs during the cooler winter and spring months and may be the best time for those wanting to stay dry on land or aboard boats to visit. Snorkelers and swimmers, on the other hand, may enjoy the summer heat.*

Another Everglades Experience

The Big Cypress National Preserve, located just north of Everglades National Park, is also part of the Everglades region. It contains many features and recreational opportunities similar to those of the national park—including hiking, boating, and fishing—but is different enough to get the attention of many Everglades visitors. It features two designated scenic drives. A 27-mile (43 km) drive cuts through cypress and pine forests, and a 17-mile (27 km) route passes by watery prairies. Big Cypress National Preserve also permits the hunting of deer, turkey, and hogs, plus the use of airboats and other off-road vehicles that are prohibited in most of Everglades National Park.

Up a Creek

Many experienced canoeists and kayakers put a good deal of planning into their Everglades trips, but that is not necessarily obvious to novices, who may decide on the spur of the moment to rent a canoe or kayak. While paddling can be an easy, relaxing form of recreation, it can also be demanding after long periods of time or if wind, weather, and tides change. Weaving through mangrove swamps can offer peaceful solitude, but becoming lost is a serious and frightening possibility. Novices are advised to keep paddling trips short and to ride tour boats to explore vast swamps or the open ocean.

Among Deceptive Predators

Alligators on land tend to appear slow and lazy, and the fact that some of them sunbathe very close to hiking trails may also make them seem docile or harmless. In actuality, these big reptiles can run quickly, and as hunters, they often remain still for long periods before attacking suddenly. Alligators are unlikely to pursue humans on land, but safe distances must be kept, and gators should never be fed. They are more dangerous in the water, where they might perceive humans as prey, and wading and swimming are prohibited in most freshwater areas of Everglades National Park.

Glossary

arboreal: describing an animal that lives in trees or relating to trees

backcountry: an area that is away from developed or populated areas

brackish: describing water that is a mixture of salt water and fresh water

coral reefs: stonelike underwater structures formed in shallow ocean waters by the buildup of dead marine organisms called coral polyps

ecosystems: communities of animals, plants, and other living things interacting together within an environment

feral: describing a domestically bred or raised animal that has returned to wild behavior

gubernatorial: describing or relating to a state governor

ice age: a period in Earth's history when temperatures were much colder and glaciers covered much of the planet

levee: a natural or artificial embankment along a river or canal that prevents floodwaters from spreading to surrounding land; a levee is also known as a dike

monocultures: areas of plant growth containing only one type of plant

nomadic: describing people who move frequently to new locations in order to obtain food, water, and shelter

peninsular: describing a strip of land projecting out from a larger land area into a body of water

raptors: birds of prey such as hawks, owls, eagles, and vultures

temperate: describing a moderate climate that lacks extreme shifts in temperature

terrestrial: describing an animal that lives on land or relating to the earth

Selected Bibliography

Cerulean, Susan, ed. *The Book of the Everglades*. Minneapolis: Milkweed Editions, 2002.

Jewell, Susan D. *Exploring Wild South Florida: A Guide to Finding the Natural Areas and Wildlife of the Everglades and Florida Keys*. Sarasota, Fla.: Pineapple Press, 2002.

Lodge, Thomas E. *The Everglades Handbook: Understanding the Ecosystem*. Boca Raton, Fla.: CRC Press, 2005.

National Geographic Guide to the National Parks of the United States. Washington, D.C.: National Geographic Society, 2009.

Our Inviting Eastern Parklands: From Acadia to the Everglades. Washington, D.C.: National Geographic Society, 1994.

Schullery, Paul. *America's National Parks: The Spectacular Forces That Shaped Our Treasured Lands*. New York: DK Publishing, 2001.

White, Mel. *Complete National Parks of the United States*. Washington, D.C.: National Geographic Society, 2009.

Websites

Everglades National Park
http://www.nps.gov/ever/index.htm
The official National Park Service site for the Everglades is the most complete online source for information on the park and includes a natural resources center.

National Geographic: Everglades National Park
http://travel.nationalgeographic.com/travel/national-parks/everglades-national-park/
This site provides a concise visitor's guide to the Everglades, complete with maps, photos, sightseeing suggestions, and links to other popular national parks.

Index